BOUND

Other Books by Ian Gouge

Novels and Novellas

The Red Tie - Coverstory books, 2024
17 Alma Road - Coverstory books, 2024
Tilt - Coverstory books, 2023
Once Significant Others - Coverstory books, 2023
On Parliament Hill - Coverstory books, 2021
A Pattern of Sorts - Coverstory books, 2020
The Opposite of Remembering - Coverstory books, 2020
At Maunston Quay - Coverstory books, 2019
An Infinity of Mirrors - Coverstory books, 2018 (2nd ed.)
The Big Frog Theory - Coverstory books, 2018 (2nd ed.)
Losing Moby Dick and Other Stories - Coverstory books, 2017

Short Stories

Dust, dancing - Coverstory books, 2024
An Irregular Piece of Sky - Coverstory books, 2023
Degrees of Separation - Coverstory books, 2018
Secrets & Wisdom - Paperback, 2017

Poetry

Grimsby Docks - Coverstory books, 2024
Crash - Coverstory books, 2023
not the Sonnets - Coverstory books, 2023
Selected Poems: 1976-2022 - Coverstory books, 2022
The Homelessness of a Child - Coverstory books, 2021
The Myths of Native Trees - Coverstory books, 2020
First-time Visions of Earth from Space - Coverstory books, 2019
After the Rehearsals - Coverstory books, 2018
Punctuations from History - Coverstory books, 2018
Human Archaeology - Paperback, 2017
Collected Poems (1979-2016) - KDP, 2017

Non-Fiction

Shrapnel from a Writing Life - Coverstory books, 2022

IAN GOUGE

BOUND

First published in paperback format by
Coverstory books, 2024

ISBN 978-1-7384693-4-5

Copyright © Ian Gouge 2024

The right of Ian Gouge to be identified as
the author of this work has been asserted
by them in accordance with the
Copyright, Designs and Patents Act
1988.

The cover image was designed by the
author using the Adobe suite of products
© Ian Gouge, 2024

All rights reserved.

No part of this publication may be
reproduced, circulated, stored in a system
from which it can be retrieved, or
transmitted in any form without the prior
permission of the publisher in writing.

www.iangouge.substack.com

www.iangouge.com

www.coverstorybooks.com

Contents

Foreword 3

*

Bound 5

Fret 25

Fish Fingers..31

Lunch, unpacked..37

Mirror 43

A Glass of Bourbon..55

Tally 69

Thursday morning..77

Crash..91

Beyond the Curtain..125

*

Acknowledgements 154

Foreword

The poetic monologues in *Bound* are the unspoken thoughts of individuals who find themselves in situations in which they are somehow tied or trapped. In their own way, each 'speaker' attempts to come to terms with their situation, to reconcile themselves with it, and — in some cases — perhaps find a way out.

Echoing some of the work of Samuel Beckett and T.S. Eliot, the poems are designed both to be read off the page and delivered on stage as dramatic monologues. The final piece in the collection, *Crash: the last 30 minutes of a life*, was performed at the Ripon Theatre Festival in June, 2023:

> "A very moving piece of performance poetry. Beautifully executed with fabulous imagery. Thought-provoking, soul-baring, and delivered with such poignancy and realism that it left a lasting impression."

> "*Crash* is impressive solo story-telling, a dramatic homage to T.S. Eliot that counts down the last minutes and seconds of a man's life. It is thoroughly enjoyable both as writing and performance."

> "A meticulously-crafted flow of images and ideas that was both absorbing and intriguing."

> "Ian Gouge commanded the sell-out audience seated in the vault at the Ripon Festival with his performance of *Crash*. His highly original poem, with hints of Dylan Thomas and Milton, was more than a reading: Ian's acting gave life to the stanzas and the spaces around them."

Although appearing on the page as contemporary free verse, the poems in *Bound* are written in something of a hybrid fashion, having the potential to be reformatted into a more formal script or even as stream-of-consciousness fiction. This flexibility is a deliberate attempt to blur the borders between genres.

This edition presents the pieces in their 'poetic' form, and each is prefaced with an indication as to how the monologue might be staged. In all cases the intention is to keep any staging as sparse as possible, and only in the final poem, "Beyond the Curtain", is there the potential for a second actor. If performed, throughout each monologue there may be the requirement for movement, gesture etc., and whilst it would have been entirely feasible to include such low-level instruction in the text, I have decided not to interrupt the flow of the poems with such asides.

Ian Gouge, 2024

Bound

The Setting

The stage is bare with the exception of a small desk and an upright chair which is set at the desk. A second upright chair is across the other side of the stage.

On the desk there is a laptop computer, a notebook, and a pen.

The stage is not brightly lit. When open, there is a glow coming from the laptop screen (which may be simulated).

Throughout the performance, the actor may stand, walk between chairs, gesture to the laptop or notebook when speaking.

The actor addresses their words to the audience partly as if they are talking to themselves, and partly as if in one-to-one conversation.

Bound

i

when evening calls
when night tightens its stranglehold
on the remnants of the day
so lights go on across the waking world

even here

we cling to what we can see
or have seen
afraid of the invisible
silently pray that these   inadequate lumens
will save us from the awesome darkness
and what we might find there

and me

i am compelled
to scratch out some kind of history
with this pen   in this book
a shield of sorts
against the coming night

ha!

and later
when i have a page or three

which — as they say — "pass muster"
i will commit my semi-adroit words
to this other god
gateway to the invisible   intangible
where collective wisdom
persuades us they will be safe
beyond the perishing of notebooks

and there
— in accordance with immortal hope —
to perhaps be future-mined
by some well-meaning curator
who might just stumble
upon my dust-dry trench
on their way to somewhere legendary

for now at least
this additional glow is welcome
comforting even
like meeting an old friend
in a darkened stairwell
and finding they are armed with a torch
all the better for seeing
against a stumble

or is that just fancy

i have no more control over this   thing
than i do the night

if i kid myself i'm in charge
it's bravado indulged by the illusion of fake knowledge

listen to my fingers on these keys
and all for
the pretence of making words dance to my tune

you don't have to look hard
to find people addicted to this   veneer of living
casting their voices into the void
sharing pictures of dogs and cats
asking inane questions
in some desperate attempt
to garner shallow acquaintance

if you were an animal what would you be (they ask)
or
what's your favourite colour
how do you take your coffee
have you ever done anything you're ashamed of
do you have a secret

and thousands answer

not i
not publicly
not wishing to expose myself to ridicule
or honesty

but here and now
to you

an owl   or a weasel
green
black and strong
yes
yes

how was that
do you feel enriched for the knowing
have you an enhanced image of me
are your mind's pixels any sharper

and me
do i feel better
for divulging such things

do you ever wonder whether
those   inquisitors   read all our answers

or if they did what that would tell them

nothing of any meaning
in such a cacophony

their interest is not in words but numbers
of responses
of likes
of shares

it's a measurement of sorts i suppose

while in the background
the black heart of the algorithm
processes a little faster
weaving its webs ever-tighter

increasingly sophisticated webs
over which we've no control
and into which we blithely walk
— day and night —
our fingers' tapping on keys
like the sound of footsteps
marching to the spider's gallows

fuck them!

for their traps
for holding us in thrall
for knowing me as well as they do

perhaps better than i do myself

ii

not for the want of trying

i say
it's not for the want of trying
me attempting to know me better

as if by doing so i will gift myself a key
a code
some magic cypher
to unlock universal secrets

not of that   thing
nor the algorithms at its black heart
but perhaps enough to scratch away at the veneer
    just a little
to be able to stand back and offer
not a glimpse
but the sliver of a glimpse

or a sliver of a sliver of a glimpse

to claim i have earned it
there's the prize

to have been validated just enough
to have the right to say
here is a morsel of the truth

can you see it

i have peeled back what i could
(and paid the price for doing so)
and here
in this book
in these words
(which are not here but rather

nestling in the black heart of the web)
is at least a clue
    or at best a clue

to be examined
roughly caressed by an archaeologist's brush
taken apart and rebuilt
reengineered (if that is more your thing)

or if not a clue in the words themselves
then somewhere between the words
in the liminal spaces

why do spaces always need to be liminal

it is a trend
do you not think

a fashion

words are slaves to fashion
have their sell-by date
a shelf-life

ha!

do you remember when paradigm was a word
worth repeating in casual conversation

now it is hackneyed
devoid of merit

soon liminal will go that way too

give me the clever ancient slippery words
that sway in the breeze of culture
fitting the purpose of time like
the fingers of a glove

gay was happy
gay was bright and cheerful
and now gay is filled with sex
because that is where we focus
in our over-complex oh so sophisticated modernity

we are masters of prejudice
without needing a qualification to prove as much

in our landscape
words are laid before us
like landmines variously disguised
(or not disguised at all)

say this but not that
that but not this

the learned will tell you
to ignore the author's intent
that it is irrelevant

but what if how we read their words today
is divorced from what they meant
when they were written

no
forget i said that

it is too knotty a problem
for a shallow mind like mine
better leave that conundrum to the smart ones
whose definition of meaning
and truth
and beauty
requires a theory and a treatise
couched in a metalanguage
reserved for the chosen few

and no   again
i shouldn't say that either
it sounds bitter
it devalues me
labels me a second-class citizen
makes me want to unpick myself
syllable by syllable
and then throw all the syllables into the air
just to see where they fall

gaily into the liminal spaces perhaps
if only for today

iii

was it always like this

a valid question
should you wish to ask it

but then again
forgive me if i seek to qualify

was *what* always like *what*

this room
the way the light falls upon flat surfaces
the shadows cast
the inadequacy of that same light
(or its adequacy
depending on your point of view)

or do you mean this notebook
just here
its pages
the words written on those pages

or this   thing
connected to the dark heart

or the dark heart itself
and being tethered to it

or does your question seek to decode
if not the words themselves
(even liminal   should you find it)
but rather how they were written
the flow of the hand
that expressive finish on a 'g'
(where it exists)

or is none of that the 'what'

perhaps you are asking about
                    shall we call it truth
the scraping at the veneer
the search for a code
the attempt to use one medium or another
    the notebook   the black heart
to get at something important

but then again
it could be none of those things
nothing of my imagining
given 'was it always like this'
is such an open-ended question
don't you think

your 'it' may not be my 'it'
your 'this' not my 'that'

ha!

the knots we tie ourselves in
as soon as
— or even before —
we have committed pen to paper
or fingers to keys

so you see the problem

was it always like this

yes or no
depending

ah
depending on what
(now we're getting somewhere!)

answer me that
because that informs the context
(context
like the man who wrote 'gay' and meant cheerful
though we assumed the other)

let me tell you what i think
— for what i think is surely
that which i wish you to know —

it depends on time
    and history

it depends on the intersections
of unrelated consequences
drawn together for the briefest of moments
by me here and you there
and between us
a constellation of words
each one accurate or inaccurate
filled with or devoid of meaning
words woven into the black heart
or onto the lines of that notebook
where the meaning is

where

'read between the lines' they say

that's as good a place as any
I suppose

iv

if i tell you my history
all those incidents which brought me here
every insignificant or nuanced encounter
      feeling
      question
      action
would it help

perhaps you might understand
why i chose this word rather than that
why i have 'a thing' about 'liminal'
why i declaim or mourn or celebrate

and if you
(to ensure the exchange was fair
and kept in balance)
told me of your history
the encounters and feelings and so forth
perhaps then we might
between us
in collaboration as it were
come to an agreement
as to what we mean by

was it always like this

even if it's just the beginning of understanding
at least it would be something to give us a hint
as to what we might replace 'it' and 'this' with

what do you think

might that work

should i sit back down
and begin to recount my life
from the earliest memory
of being a child in a small terraced house

it would be a journey measured in time
height-marked in pencil on a wall
or by the failing of eyesight
or the breaking of a heart
(more than once)

and if you did the same

in the end
what would we have
collaboratively created

an understanding

would you trade all that effort for the instant
when you might say

ah   i see

iv

don't kid yourself

there are too many constraints
to offer us such possibilities

constraints and inadequacies

and if we see
here or in the dark heart

in words or the spaces between them
(the elasticity of the web!)
sufficient flexibility to reward us with illusion
the sense that we can make sense
and explain and share and even   understand
then that is part of the trap too

i am bound by this
          and this   and this
i am taunted
challenged by
their silent persuasion

someone who once wrote liminal
and thought she knew what it meant
confessed to delusion

sometimes i think i'm deluding myself
she said

we do
we have to
words are the handmaidens of delusion
not of understanding

we dare not stare into the heart of the web
nor at the bonds which anchor us there
and so we fabricate
like piping pink icing atop a cake
made of cardboard

we stand back to admire our handiwork
its appeal
we salivate at the way the colours compliment
(or clash)
convince ourselves that we have reached out
that there is someone prepared
to grasp our hand in gratitude

that there is understanding

or a glimmer of understanding
or the sliver of a glimmer
or the sliver of a sliver

unable to shake these bonds
knowing they cannot be loosed
we are forced into accepting
delusion is life

that in the end
we are as bound to our delusions
as we are to the dark heart
and its ministering algorithms

i would ask you what then is left
but the question is inevitably rhetorical
rhetorical and universal
and so
in order to avoid your demand
to categorically resolve

'was it always like this'

i sit in this poor light
permit night to follow day
devote myself to the inadequacies of language

almost certain
that we are tied ever-tighter
to the web

that our faith grows ever-weaker
as our delusion grows ever-stronger

that i can never convey what it is you wish to know
nor what i want to tell you

that somewhere untouchable
— even in the liminal spaces! —
is that which we truly seek

that today will be as yesterday was
and tomorrow as today

until that final mute-enforced time
when after one last night there are no more days
and all uncertainties dissolve
and the answer to the question
was it always like this
is discovered

Fret

The Setting

The location is a back-stage dressing room at a theatre/music venue.

At the very minimum there needs to be some kind of table with a mirror on it, a chair at the table, and, propped up on a stand near one of the wings, an electric guitar.

The vast majority of the dialogue is delivered sitting down, directly to the audience (with the odd reference to the mirror). The piece could end with the actor moving to collect the guitar and then walking off-stage.

Fret

you can hear them outside
punctuated by the rhythmic drumbeat
that travels from the strobe-lit stage
to permeate the walls of stark passageways
and arrive at these rooms
rooms with stars painted on the doors

even though they are happy
dancing
clapping
i know they are here for me
that the soon crescendo of their cheers
will be part-appreciation
part-expectation

most of them know the routine
the queue for the loos
the bar
while the stagehands earn their corn
and the roadies soundcheck once more
against some banal backing track
bordering on the unacceptable

someone said they had shakespeare here last week

there would have been applause then too
even cheering
who knows

but it would have been understated
metaphorical almost
not like the rawness of tonight
people grateful you almost made their ears bleed

bubble bubble toil and trouble

when it goes quiet
when the timbre of the sound changes
when i can hear footsteps outside
nervous laughter from the rest of the band
then i know there are just a few minutes until
i sling the fender over my shoulder
and begin the slow march to the stage

it is a walk i know too well
have made so many times before
not here perhaps
but what's the difference

a walk where i transform myself
from who i am
to the person they want me to be

i rewind myself like an old cassette
and press play
then listen to the old familiar sounds

maybe it's all just muscle memory now
for me

and the fender
and the guys

i talked about mixing it up
a new riff on old tunes
playing with the lyrics
leaving out the hits
even the ancient ones

but i was outvoted
all was inviolable

*give the people what they want
and they'll keep coming back*

but for how much longer

i can restring a guitar
force it back into tune
good as new
no-one any the wiser

but what about me

my strings are lose
my fretboard's beginning to warp
i'm not the person i was
not that younger guy the audience
will soon convince themselves
they are seeing yet again

Fish Fingers

The Setting

This piece is set at a supermarket checkout. At the very least, therefore, there should be a long table to represent the conveyor belt. One end of this should probably be set close to the edge of the stage and almost at right angles to it. The actor would sit at the far end of the table near a till (if one is sourced).

The actor remains sitting at the till throughout. She looks out into the audience as if looking out into the store itself — except for a brief sideways glance when referring to her colleague.

fish fingers

i

a quiet moment
the conveyor belt empty
like an oasis in a sandstorm

yet there they all are
still trolley-pushing
shuffling the aisles
archaeologists searching for treasure

some come armed with lists
as if these were maps
x marks the spot
others plod on autopilot
or bustle randomly

you get to know them
the types

when they find out you are local
or when you've smiled at them
or helped with out with something unbarcoded
when you've defused their embarrassment
at having done a silly thing
they show their gratitude
by seeking you out
next time they come

as if that's what you want
that kind of reward
rather than this

the empty belt
a moment to yourself

ii

two tills away
cheryl's quiet too

hating inefficiency
soon they'll pull one of us off
to go out back
or stack shelves
or take our break early

at their beck and call
always

for the first time in ages
i notice the tannoy
its tinny bark demanding assistance
in aisle seven
probably another bottle of sherry
knocked from the shelf

the whiff of oloroso
can last longer than you think

you can always tell the guilty ones

as you can tell the ones ready to pay

either they emerge from an aisle
steely-eyed
determined
focussed on us
or
trolley already full
they'll be casting about
for something they've missed
panicking over walnuts
or caster sugar

list or no list

iii

these things pinned to us are no help
bright plastic squares
into which our names have been routered
gifting us to them
to be addressed familiarly
even without our permission

sorry sharon love
but i've picked one up without a label
how much is it

too much as it turned out

there it sits by my till
like a castaway awaiting rescue
to be returned
back to the shelf for a second chance
or ditched in the charity bins out back

cast away
in fact

i think about tom hanks
just for a second
just long enough to miss the elderly couple
heading to the top of my belt
pausing apologetically
as they take the first item from their trolley
divesting themselves of it
long enough for me to pick it up
scan it
a 10-pack of fish fingers
then pass it back

but even before then the training kicks in

hello
how are you
looks a bit dismal outside

Lunch, unpacked

The Setting

Set at the seaside, minimal staging would require a long bench facing squarely towards the audience and upon which the actor sits. Their points of reference are the audience (where they imagine the gull to be), and then off in the direction in which their companion has temporarily departed.

The only prop that might be required is something to represent their lunch which at first they hold, and then later place on the bench.

The attack by the gull will obviously be harder to manifest. Is the lunch packaging somehow pulled from the bench at the decisive moment? Perhaps from off-stage somehow?

Or there is no physical representation of the lunch, and the action is mimed (perhaps with sudden sound effects)?

Lunch, unpacked

the seagull watches
weighing-up its options
marks the arc made by the chip
on its journey from greasy paper to my mouth

it could choose to strike at any moment

arm against this sun-baked wall
a sea breeze rustles the paper
the bird's feathers

it shifts a little to the left
a little closer

did i ever know they were so large

i want to check where jay is
if he's on his way back with the coffees
the trace of him left beside me
is the crumpled flotsam of his lunch
which the bird has eyed too
perhaps assuming i cannot guard two things at once

we both watch and wait
knowing something will happen

because something has to

not with this gull who
we both know
will win in the end
but with jay
because of his declaration

it had been a while coming
brewing courage he said
yet it landed in a rush
descending from somewhere unseen
just like the gull
to suddenly be square before me
his question

does he want my answer when he returns
an answer crafted from thin air

surely i had been expecting it
his own expectation

is getting coffee
an excuse to give me time
(a ridiculous notion in itself)
or to bestow the same on himself
to regather or calm down
or whatever else he needs to do

pee probably

yet here i am
challenged by this steely-eyed bird
who waits for me to make just one false move
trapping me against this wall
cradling the remains of lunch
unable to avoid its eye
or think of anything else

perhaps i should just give in

sacrificing myself
i place what's left of mine next to jay's
push the wrappers away to the right
disowning the last few chips
then shifting to the left
double the distance
make the invitation

come on then

the gull shuffles a little
eyes the prize suspiciously
as if a trap has been laid

i need it to be gone
to have this over with
so i can focus

then
when i edge left again
everything happens in an instant

the flurry of wings
still makes me jump
the sound
its size
for a moment
i could reach out
brush its feathers with my hand
make a connection
confirm permission

and then it is away
and as i follow the beginning of its flight
i catch sight of jay heading back
the slightly shy wave of his hand
a look that is far from predatory

i know he will ask about the bird
the chips
whether i am untroubled
and i will say yes
shift slightly left again
contemplate another decision

MIRROR

The Setting

This is set in a bathroom or bedroom. As such, the only prop required is the mirror.

Given the actor addresses much of her words to the mirror (standing up), it needs to be located between her and audience in such as way to allow her to be seen by the audience — and for the mirror itself not to obscure their view.

Some thought should probably be given as to when in the day the action occurs; obviously either first thing in the morning or last thing at night is most likely. This will effect how the actor is dressed, the stage is lit etc.

Mirror

i

whose is this narrow face
staring back
accusation in the eyes
or regret
or recognition

or lack of it

like wearing glasses with the wrong prescription
squinting blurs its edges
and when i do
i see her reflected back

it's uncanny this   duplication
being sprung from the same mould
a physical form carrying the imprint of history
       of legacy
       of betrayal
and telling the world not everything about who you are
(although the world might assume that)
but some part of where you came from
her history overlaid on yours
like thin and crinkled carbon paper
you would consign to the bin
as if in doing so the past might go too
wipe the dna-slate clean

allow you to look in the mirror
and say

this is me

not
this is my mother's daughter

ii

when i was still a child
i did childish things
played in the park
invented games with my friends

fantasy was my motto

if we watched films to pass the time
movies nurtured that in me too

perhaps one day
or for more than one day
i was dorothy
with my bright red shoes
toto the dog i could never have

how we skipped the yellow road
not cowardly nor made of tin or straw
until in a momentary glance
perhaps a single frame

smuggled inside a scene
that narrow face

and in that face i saw and knew
my mother was the wicked witch
come from the west's dusk
and into my life to taunt and torture me

she never left

she is here still
not close   but close enough
not dead   but alive enough
i can feel her malevolence
as it travels the motorways
silently traverses the train tracks
i can hear her whispering accusations
that nagging voice
asserting my inadequacy

arm's length is not far enough
nor is another city
another county

and sometimes
when i am least expecting it
i see her again

the wicked witch of the west
glaring out of the mirror

iii

they ring me with updates
the staff paid to care
though how do you care for a witch

interesting how time has warped their tone
the slide away from the upbeat
away from encouragement
the positive picture they were painting
probably inaccurate   unrealistic
more impressionistic than anything
as if i would fall for the soft colours
the magic trick they were trying to pull
verbal sleight of hand

come
they were saying
she wants to see you
they were saying

standard patter bestowed on the absent
all the while hoping to pass the baton
for an hour or two
to give them a chance for a chat
put their feet up
have a fag

after all we've earned it

don't think i haven't noticed
how over time the tone hardened
the messages from the front-line less optimistic

i threw filters onto the phone
and picked out their anger
disappointment
disapproval

theirs
as well as hers

but i've done my time
i want to say
i'm a fully paid-up member
even if i never wanted to be
i have the scars
see them every time i look in the mirror
so why can't you

because you're never here

perhaps less than fellow-feeling
as much as anything their desperation is for relief
triggering a panoply of excuses
as i navigated further from the truth

but they have their own filters too
i'm sure of that
we've heard it all before

they never said
but thought it

so in the end i gave them silence
listened without hearing
when they called
i took the phone to the bathroom
and stared at myself as they spoke
to remind me
why i hadn't gone for weeks
why i didn't care

and all the while i stared at me
so she did too

i see the bitch every day
i wanted to say

i don't need to be there

iv

i wanted to be snow white
live that crude rural idyll
so why shouldn't i have seen her in the mirror
a physical manifestation of Disney's beauty
raven-dark hair
red lips beyond red
etcetera
etcetera

mirror mirror on the wall

no prizes for guessing who i did see

freud would have a field day
the only people i ever wanted to be
fictional creations
tied to the black hearts of witches

v

her soul probably needs it more than mine
but confession they say

you know the rest

i chose to move this far away
a gap measured in hundreds not tens
to introduce impossibility
so that i couldn't just hop on a bus
or jump on a train
so that i could take myself out of the equation
cancelled out on both sides of the equals sign

lowest common denominator she'd probably say

just what i'd expect

i absented myself so i didn't have to bear witness
leave some poor third party

paid to disentangle her from her life's detritus
the ornaments and mementos
photographs of other people
souvenirs of other lives
anyone's but mine

handing the money over was easy
an antiseptic transaction
my inverted version of judas with
no attendant unpleasantness

absence and the heart's fondness
another myth

vi

what would make a difference
what would transform my mirrored experience
and return the bathroom cabinet
to its right and proper purpose

don't think i haven't thought about it

her carers have hinted at forgiveness
though coy about where responsibility lay
who makes the first move
and in their thinly veiled way
they have suggested she is ready
but to speak or to listen
that's the question

a world of difference between the two

and the unspoken presumption
that i too might be ready

to listen or speak

they suggest the recovery of lost harmony
is just one visit away
as if there is a magic wand to be waved
to erase the years of demands
and abuse
of victimisation
and punishment
of failing to live up to an impossible standard

or stoop down to it

are slates ever wiped clean

i think not
and in thinking not so i disqualify their premise
there is nothing she could say
or i could hear
which would be salve enough

yes
i tell them
i will visit
but only once more

and on my terms
when there is no need to listen
because she will be unable to speak
and armed with black bags
i will go through her things
not with any desire to rescue
but to expunge
for there is nothing i want from that putrid little oasis
her room in a bungalow of purgatory

nothing

other than space
the space vacated by her
the silence from telephone calls not made
from requests i no longer need to deny

and after that
when i return home
i will take down my bathroom cabinet
smash its mirror
put a new one up in its place

A Glass of Bourbon

The Setting

Set in a hotel bar, minimal staging would be a stool on which the actor sits throughout. Immediately in front of the stool is a high table upon which there should be a number of empty glasses.

The actor should face into the audience i.e. the table is between he and they. The empty glasses may be used as 'prompts' at the end of each section. If so, there should be one glass per section; the actor should not reference the same glass more than once.

A Glass of Bourbon

i

have you noticed
how ice changes the colour of a drink
dilutes burnt umber
turns ochre to pale yellow

appropriate i suppose
given the accompanying dilution
of strength
of warmth

i have never known
nor could imagine
someone wanting ice in their drink
for anything other than to make it cold

this scotch is too strong barman
put some ice in it

i mean
why would you

and there is something else
esoteric
enchanting
the way the ice in the water
diffuses the light

scatters it in all directions
especially in certain environments

like here

and the glass in front of me
the one i play with
the fingers of my left hand caressing it
the chill of the crystal
and when i turn the glass
squat and heavy-bottomed
the light moves with the ice
like a symphony
hypnotising

i could watch ice dissolve in booze for hours

in theory anyway
if that was all i did with it
just watch
but it's never in the glass for long enough
gone before the ice has had the opportunity
to fully melt

i tell myself that
it's as much about embarking on that journey
(watching the dissolving of ice)
as it is about anything else
knowing that is not true

perhaps once it was
but not now

i lift the glass from the counter
drain the contents

same again

ii

the bar is dark
chunks of wood stained and polished
cleverly fused together
to give the impression of one massive slab
whether or not there could ever be a tree
so broad and true

if you look closely
run your fingers across its surface
you find small fissures
here and there
clues as to inherent fractures
that all is not as it appears
even if it oozes quality

as does the lighting
gentle spots onto the wood
brighter behind the bar
enough to make the mirrors shine

the phalanx of bottles arranged like soldiers
    alluring
    enticing
their various ordinance
    clear
        golden
            dark as pitch
promising experience in abundance

like alice at the tea-party perhaps

but i am more pragmatic now
have taken their measure
i know what i like

just as i like this bar in this hotel
my twice-monthly refuge for how long now
long enough for the bar staff to know me
my preferences
both before and after dinner
i daresay someone in an office
beyond one of those heavy oak doors
knows the limits of my expense account
what i can get away with

superficial stuff
knowing someone has a penchant
for after-dinner bourbon
and licence for a forty-quid-a-night expenses tab
food included

not that it was always bourbon
but just recently
and just here
a kind of badge worn to suggest cachet
a signal for anyone on the lookout
for someone who might be just a little different
a little more interesting
not just a businessman on a jolly

as if

same again

iii

i've no-one to answer to except me
there's no card being marked elsewhere
no tally
no points
i share my conscience with no-one but myself
not any more

you might argue the bottle is my conscience
hell
i might argue that too
my conscience and my confessor
that which absolves me
every time i arrive at the bottom of a glass

forgive me bourbon for i have sinned

or beaujolais or chardonnay
or a nice east-coast single malt
one of the expensive ones

all priests in variously stained vestments
but with the same purpose
the same connections
one might say

yet how can a one-way conversation be a connection

i've found that out
and did so the hard way
pain which nothing glass-bottomed could soothe
no compensation in ice's splitting of light
no rainbowed beams to soften the anguish

light dancing through liquid was merely that
scientific fragmentation
not attributes of prismatic beauty
like antiseptic diagrams taken from a textbook
and made real

hard-edged
i was immune
miracle or marvel
i remained unmoved

you were always the one who led me there
parted the curtains of the mundane
allowed me to see what lay beyond

in those days the wine was shared
almost a celebration
but now each glass is a salute
that's what i tell myself
or homage
because i have found no other way
because the way i have found serves many purposes
yet only one master

the ice in this glass shifts as it melts
catches a spotlight on the bar
because that is where i have placed it
where the magic happens
or where numbness might triumph
if i wait long enough

same again

iv

once
not so long ago
i got talking to a woman
three stools along from here
before we moved to a table in the corner
low with easy chairs

where the lighting went down a notch
and nothing sparkled in the glass
i forget the circumstance
the trigger that broke the ice as it were
that prompted me to offer to buy her a drink
and for her to accept it

vodka and orange
lots of ice

the talk flowed
as the rounds ticked-off the evening
getting the measure of each other
the unspoken profiling
assessments born from too many nights
alone in hotel bars

well
certainly in my case

until that moment when silence fell
for the first time in two hours
requiring calculations to be made
the next move suddenly become a thing
as if it had been hiding behind our soft chairs
all the white awaiting its chance
to spring out
surprise us
even if we'd known it had been there all along

her room
my room
our rooms

she excused herself and didn't come back

perhaps that was her answer
not verbalised
but undeniably potent

and the barman came over to the table
examined me there on my own
with raised eyebrows drawing his own conclusion

same again

v

or perhaps it was my history that drove the wedge
immutable and untouchable

did i talk of you

would she have asked
isn't that a standard gambit
to find a way to slip into conversation

and what does your wife do

or something similar

and if she had
what would i have said
standard lines designed to fit circumstance
a crude disguise
the truth with shades on

she died

    or she's dead to me

she left me

    or she died

our lives have gone in different directions

all driven by the tone I wanted to strike
big on sympathy
or the opposite
keen to assert my independence
that i can be my own man

does it make any difference
to anyone else that is
people ask but they don't care
and those who know don't ask
because they have no need
the picture already filled-in
like a paint-by-numbers

if so
i may have strayed over the lines once or twice

but you
not here
nor waiting at home when i get back
no more gentle debates about shopping lists
presents at christmas
where to go on holiday
the colour we should paint the kitchen

not there
for me to recount my trip
the good and bad of work
successes and failures however minor
or major

not here or there
as if delivering on a promise
that one day you'd prove how much i needed you

same again

the barman is benevolent
we have an understanding after all this time

don't you think you've had enough sir

oh
more than you could ever know

TALLY

The Setting

The stage is bare apart from the frame of a voting booth which stands front and centre. Only part of the booth's sides are extant, along with a small shelf (audience-side) on which sits a single sheet of paper and a small black crayon.

The actor stands at the booth facing the audience. They hold the crayon in their fingers until they make their mark and leave the stage.

They are about to cast their vote.

Tally

i

the black crayon is child-fodder fat
too crude to permit subtle expression
but that's no matter
given all they want
is a scrawl in one of two boxes

'x' marks the spot

i would i had my penknife
to whittle away at the point
to refine it
       stray toward elegance
as if that might allow the mark i make
to be something other

but it sits
       the knife
on my kitchen table
me knowing about body searches
the need for security
after one voter's crazed rampage
four years ago

if people need to die
it should not have to be the innocent

but i should not say that
or think it
i should be grateful there is a choice
even if three-quarters of the votes cast
          the 'x' placed in the lower box
will be destroyed before counting

destroyed before counting
but not until after they have cross-referenced
the number on the slip
with the voters' register

one black mark leading to another
which leads to what

there is   some say
a tally kept
      under lock-and-key
           behind a firewall
a tally of black marks
constantly checked against a threshold
which   undefined and unknown
is conveniently flexible

one day you're a good citizen
the next

so we make our mark where we should
we keep our tally low
and live with the consequences

ii

some say
the process is the same in every country
ubiquity in the signifier
    the crayons representing it
    the small empty boxes
    the demand for an 'x'

others say
that though elsewhere there might be choice
    three
        or four
            or twelve boxes
the outcome is the same
an exercise to favour the few
each box the emblem of ambition
ambition veiled in a credo for good
        stitched together with slogans of peace
        a tapestry of promises
        the veil of security

these boxes bound a space
in which hope is supposed to be harmonised
into common purpose
        fellow-feeling
and where your cross should be etched
not merely as an 'x'
    but as a kiss
        an expression of faith

the utterance
i do

but there is nothing inside the box

some say
there is no tally in other countries
and that to make your black mark
is an expression of freedom
not a cross of denial

but that's what they would say
      we're told

pick your lie
make your mark

perhaps in some places
they might even allow you
to whittle away at the point of the crayon
with a small knife

iii

there

capitulation

now to leave
to return home

to await the results that will be delivered tomorrow
        promptly   as promised
and to watch the coverage
the analysis of the numbers
        turnout
        votes cast
        percentage split
and to realise it is the same as before
like a tv show on re-run
repeated once every four years

or a murder-mystery
where you know the guilty party
as soon as the titles roll

iv

look at this small
                squat
                        insignificant crayon
hear the hollowness of its sound
as i leave it for the next person to lift
as they consider the voting slip
its two boxes
use the crayon to make a mark
where they are supposed to

who could ever have imagined
such a small inanimate thing
        black and innocently glossy

                tactile yet slippery
could wield so much power

and i long again for my knife
not to whittle the crayon to a fine point
but to chop it into pieces
so small no-one could pick them up
the 'x' unemployed
        the square left empty
                the people freed

Thursday morning

The Setting

Although it would be possible to create an elaborate backdrop for this piece — the interior of a Post Office — it would also be entirely possible for the stage to be completely bare.

In this case the actor would start perhaps a third of the way back, and then move toward the audience incrementally as they edge to the front of the queue.

A decision will need to be made which side of the stage represents the location of the counter. It is only here the actor occasionally diverts his gaze.

Thursday morning

You are now number 4 in the queue

shuffle

shuffle

not far enough to take a proper step
progress measured in inches
time hypnotised by the shape in front of you

once it would have been overcoat
        raincoat
        duffle
now it's all black hoodies
puffed up jackets
or denims so battered
it's as if all the angels have pissed on them

that's what they say isn't it
about angels and rituals

but maybe i'm just tired
tired and grouchy
it's a trait i'm trying to nurture
                            the grouchy part
in order to comply with a stereotype
not wanting to let anyone down

ha
a joke

not grouchy at all then

but tired
of course

is the most tired me or this place
whose walls haven't seen a lick of paint since
i don't know when
    maybe when we made it
      to the quarter finals of the cup

and that shelving
a kind of knock-off cream
as if smuggled from the back of that store
the one on the high street
            filled with departments
before it was closed down

receivership
almost sounds as if someone is going to catch it
    take over
    take care
when all they do is take
take and sell
and leave nothing but a shell

not even shelves

and now that cream colour's here
like the sign of a disease   spreading

you get the colour and you're doomed
a black spot

someone should nail something to the door

and i wouldn't mind
            about this place i mean
other than there's nowhere else to go now
to get cash   pay bills

used to be you could be sure
to meet someone in here
        thursdays especially
        pension day
days when there were things
to be caught up on
        or shared
        news and gossip
        old lies to be retold

but not now

oh
hang on

You are now number 3 in the queue

the sign doesn't flash that exact message to me
not like those call-centre telephones
where some plastic voice tries to encourage you
to keep your spirits up
as you edge closer to the front of your wait

progress they call it

but here
you have to count
bodies

when someone moves away
above a vacant till a light flashes
someone new takes their place
(a guy in overalls this time)
and you shuffle on
look at your hands again
make sure you're still holding
what you were holding thirty seconds ago
pray again that you've forgotten nothing
hope you're served by diane at the end
not the spotty individual next to her
who can't stop sniffing
and wouldn't know a second class stamp
if one was pasted over his eyes

she's been here years
enough to know what we want before we get to her
is happy to chat on less busy days

which is not today

and so
number three in the queue
behind one black puffer
    and a large woman in a pink coat
    who looks like trouble
        too officious
        too many requests
        too much uncertainty

and not an ounce of common
otherwise she wouldn't wear that coat

is it any wonder you can't take
your eyes from it
unnatural pink
borrowed not from nature
but a blend   a compound of chemicals
fused from luminous atoms
                        radiant ions
tested on mice   and rabbits
and now on humans

not her
the woman thus adorned
but on the rest of us
the poor buggers who have to suffer
its intrusion on our fading eyes
as if we didn't have enough trouble
as it is

oh
hang on

You are now number 2 in the queue

diane smiles at the pink one
and i feel doomed
to suffer at the hands of the spotted youth

ahead of me
the black puffer shifts nervously
as if the balls of his feet
are treading hot coals

not feeling them myself
i have to look down
to check

perhaps it's nerves
perhaps he's not good with people
or he's excited that money is so close
assuming that's why he's here

why else

for an instant i imagine
that somewhere beneath that coat
a bomb is taped to his chest
and beneath that hood is the face of revenge
       and martyrdom
that when he makes it to the counter
he'll flick a hidden switch
                  or press a button
to settle a long-held grudge
or embrace ideology
and blow us all to kingdom come

they'd have to redecorate the place then

i catch the beginning of a smile
thrown by this incongruous notion
and then chase it away
with realisation that I wouldn't miss it
       the post office
or miss myself   come to that
my smithereens decorating the market square

perhaps some of them
                       whatever they might be
would be blown all the way to the churchyard
where god knows i'll be soon enough
where i should have been for a while now
reunited

was a time when i'd be here with peg
her handbag the cavernous void
into which our cards
          and letters
          and bills
     would all be subsumed
     until we made it to the till
days when i didn't need to worry
about what i had in my hand
     what i might have left at home
     if i'd forgotten anything
days when i was allowed to be absent-minded
because she had the reins
and i was just riding shotgun

that was a phrase i used
too many years ago now to count
     riding shotgun
born from my love of westerns

it was meant to make her feel secure
that i had her back
we were a team

it made her laugh at first
years later she'd just roll her eyes

there was a world of history in that gesture

and now here i am
at number two
my natural place in the scheme of things
when peg was number one

oh
hang on

You are now number 1 in the queue

the guy in the dungarees
slouches towards the exit
and the puffer-bomber makes it to the counter

i wait a few seconds
for the bang
for nothingness

did i just close my eyes

when i look
his hood is down
and he seems a normal young man
even the spotty one is cracking a smile
so he must have said something funny

or perhaps knows him

there is an exchange
    documents
    cards
    money

next door
the pink coat leans close to the screen
as if her message to diane
is top secret   somehow unique

surely this will make diane's day
serving someone so pink

ahead of me a rack of greetings cards
and assorted tat
strategically placed
one last temptation

i look down at my feet
wanting to see a line in the matting
a stop sign
but there is none of course
and i feel from behind
the weight of impatience
the eyes of others who long
to be where i am

number one

who finishes first
pink or puffer

i want to place a bet with myself
but don't know who to choose
i wouldn't give myself
very good odds anyway

so instead i look again at my hands
how they clutch desperately
at the flotsam of this morning's transaction
        gas bill
        electric
        poll tax
        bank card

i try to remember my security code
its four digits dancing a tarantella in my head
try to recall how much it all comes to
                              these bills

it's so hard to keep track these days

a cough behind me

i look up
the display flashes
at the counter
diane smiles

CRASH

The Setting

There is a bed of some kind at the back of the stage (could be camp bed, mattress); the actor is 'asleep' on this at the opening of the piece.

Front left is a chair at a small table. On the chair is a dressing gown. On the table, a cup, a knitted or crocheted remembrance poppy, the text of *Crash* printed out on small sheets of paper (A6) fixed together somehow e.g. with a treasury tag.

Front left is another upright chair.

The piece opens with the man 'waking up'. He goes to the table and puts on his dressing gown. He notices the text of *Crash*; picks it up, slowly tears off the first few sheets until he gets to the opening words. As he performs the piece, when each page has been read, he tears it off and lets if also fall to the floor. Note: he does not read from the paper; although it can be used as an aide memoir, its primary function is to effect a form of countdown. When he utters the final word, he drops whatever is left in his hands to the floor.

During the performance he can move between the table and the two chairs as deemed appropriate.

Crash

- after re-reading T.S.Eliot

i

memory is the pattern of tweed
the old wool-work of warp and weft
stitched inside night-time eyelids
the mottled colours of recall
awaiting you when
eyes still closed
you try to rouse from sleep
and find yourself bound in the weave
the life you've woven for yourself
or life has woven about you

warp and weft
in and out

searching for pattern in the not-cloth
is like scanning an archive
for a familial tartan
something to hang on to
when all's said and done
instinctively knowing last night was

it

the final time you might have been
enchanted

memory is the only weapon
we have against death
remembering proves we're alive
even if
like raking over old coals
the cold clinker of our lives
we do nothing but generate dust
ash to be swept up
swept into a bag
disposed of in the black bin
awaiting Monday's collection

there goes my life
tossed by men in hi-vis
into the back of a grubby yellow truck
warning lights flashing

ii

there is only one journey
one filled with multiple beginnings
too many to count

and multiple endings
each deceptive
couched in the cloak of a lie
a tartan cloak
frayed at the edges
letting colour bleed out
in fragile skeins of thread

toward a future
where it might be re-woven
by you

warp and weft
in and out

or bagged and binned

we pretend glimpses of conclusion
pretend we understand
like that car shooting a red light
the skid outside the restaurant
tyre-tracks on the road
lines woven into the story

while inside
at the counter   waiters
wait

waved to our table
they saunter over
flourish a plastic menu

voices of temptation

suggest the dish-of-the-day
as if it were a gem
hewn from rock
by a back-broken miner

pausing for our order
he has no interest in beginnings
or endings
only to avoid rebuke
to ensure the pattern on his waistcoat
is aligned
lines and lies peddled
to keep the punters happy

that night could have been
the last time we were

enchanted

at the foot of the menu
in small print
ghosted on natty paper to chime
with the waiters' waistcoats
usual warnings about allergies
disclaimers about the presence
(or absence)
of nuts
statements on the dangers of

self-consumption

the maître d'
replete with recipes
a taste for the obtuse
has a story he likes to tell

about beginnings
and an apple

don't think about the man
think about the bite
and ask
who is there
to make the apple whole again

beginnings and endings
woven into the fabric of his words too
words hiding behind
the lids of his eyes
in the warp and weft
of skeins and veins

iii

under an immeasurable canvas
an illiterate juggler practices still
the necks of his clubs
worn thin by decades of
throwing
catching
dropping
starting again

ask him
and he'll tell you he's just beginning
to get the hang of it after all this time

listen closely
and hear him count

sixty-two   sixty-three   sixty-four

as the heavy clubs
pirouette in the air
slip from one hand to the next
like a cheap trick
you're not supposed to notice
eyes fixed on those above his head
wondering if they're high enough
spinning enough

wondering if he's going to let one fall
when he's going to let one fall

sixty-five   sixty-six   thump

chipped enamel flakes into a pattern
not unlike tweed
(or unlike tweed)
crazed like veins
yet the clubs remain what they have always been
hard and solid and unyielding
even in the light's deception
when spinning in the air

or falling to the floor

iv

soon it will be the time of poppies
knitted to railings
crocheted on lampposts
little balloons of red and black

like signposts
both to the past
and the future
poppies woven into the warp and weft
of time

and next time
if there is a next time
if we can find a way
to make it be the last time
what colours will the poppies be
those of remembrance
multicoloured threads
knit into a kind of tartan
almost regular
precise
but not quite
because that is the nature of wool

to be slack
and imprecise

a different kind of failure

children tug to free the poppies
as if it were a game
like 'trick or treat'
expecting a prize
a sweet
a trip to the circus to watch what

the acrobats
a lion tamer
or the juggler
struggling to find a rhythm
as if somewhere in his head
he can hear

an antique drum

beating out
as he starts again

sixty-six   sixty-five   sixty-four

and the children cheer
faces rouged by excitement
not understanding his goal
nor the meaning of poppies
only knowing
how pretty they look
sewn into the warp and weft
of the horses' tack
the tartan cloak of the ring master

sixty-three   sixty-two   sixty-one

all they want to see
are the clowns
with their flapping feet
and painted faces
the gaudy checks of over-large jackets
as if laughter has been woven in
woven into their walk
the way they fuss and push

the near collision
with the juggler

sixty   fifty-nine   fifty-eight

while outside
rain begins to batter the tent
and the canvas sags
threateningly

and no-one has the heart
to tell the children
this could be the last time
they are ever

enchanted

the juggler continues
the ancient drum beats on
and from somewhere else
just beyond

the still point

comes a sound
no-one else can hear
no-one else can interpret

fifty-seven   fifty-six   fifty-five

v

take the tea cup to the pot
or to the jug

milk first! milk first!

you watch the white spoil
make the dirty journey to brown
the tones through which it travels
cower unnameable

when did you learn
that 'builder's tea' was a shade of ochre
darker than tan
more sombre than burgundy

less threatening than peat

make it like that

you once said
as if turning colour to taste
in the fusing of senses
(or confusing them)
rejoicing in overlap
the collusion of allies
habitually bent on keeping to themselves

the knowledge of dead secrets

as if they might be parachuted-in
under cover of darkness
whispering meaningless codewords
directions taken from incomplete maps

what did you say   milk first

each sense pleads for priority
recognition
having kept its secrets far too long

fifty-four   fifty-three   fifty-two

through the open window
you imagine distant music
emanating from a circus tent in the field

and wonder to which pasture the herd
has been evicted

and when they will be back
and how many of them

beef and horseradish
I've taken the crusts off
because of your teeth

recognising the big-top tune
you play notes in your head
mesmerised by the wave of
their rise and fall
and want to imagine an orchestra
resplendently dressed
safe under the tent's canvas

but you know it to be only a vinyl recording

what was that, dear

perhaps the acrobats are practicing
interlocking hands to keep them secure
like putting words together

the weft and the warp

or the lion tamer
is cracking his whip

and realises his heart isn't in it
the same old show

even the lion looks bored

and there is the juggler

fifty-one   fifty   forty-nine

each of them with their dead secrets
knowledge of them
in locking hands
cracking whips
tossing clubs just high enough

then the music stops
leaves them frozen mid-action
the acrobat suspended in mid-air
the lion tamer's whip about to crack
the juggler's clubs about to fall

this   you think   is

the still point

or

the unattended moment

between one thing and the next
the in-betweenness
a thing in its own right

fingers an inch apart
the whip's tip an inch away
the club an inch from its apex

before

yes
milk first   please

vi

so
much later
settled into the too familiar couch
absorbed into its pattern
not unlike tweed
(or unlike tweed)
recall with increasing inaccuracy
the waiter
the voice of temptation
menu items not chosen

why not the steak

I was tempted by the ribollita

that thing with spices sounded interesting

now
laughter is served up
a side-dish defending
against the vagueness of memory

there is a beat in the struggle to recall

forty-eight   forty-seven   forty-six

something to get used to
with an ending of its own perhaps

what was it the waiter said
about the bite in the apple

was that the waiter

yes, I think so, dear

it seems so long ago

in the corner of the room
the tall clock
ticks
each tick the end of the previous
or its own beginning

forty-five   forty-four   forty-three

and silence falls   between
settles like unexpected dust
layering all our surfaces
stealing definition
from the patterns
we have woven

in and out

from somewhere
a story resurrects itself
kick-started in the vacuum

do you remember that time…

but either you do not recall
or you are scarred by memory
the warp and weft of it
unsure if
after all this time
it's really something
to hang on to
especially knowing tonight might have been
the last time you were

forty-two   forty-one   forty

and an evening fulfils its purpose
as the container of things past

vii

once
his father nagged him

you can't spend time twice

as he watched him lounging
in the intangible world of the mind

and now
and so much later
the echo returns
almost visible
shimmering as if a mirage
shape and sound just out of reach

knowing the truth of it

the tolling bell

he re-hears those words not as admonishment
but as a plea
chiselled into the fabric of everything
and from its sphinx-like mouth
whispering in the corners of the room
behind the heavy drapes

you can't spend time twice

in the armchair on which father used to sit
he sees the spectre of a ventriloquist's dummy
frozen in silence
fixed on something only it can see
or hear

thirty-nine   thirty-eight   thirty-seven

a solitary juggler in a moth-eaten tent perhaps
or the metronomic ticking of time
leaking away like
rainwater falling helplessly through a grid
away into the drain-black
and out of sight

and with the water
flow secrets
and history
the wisdom that made his father say

you can't spend time twice

paralysed by partial understanding
old words make him ache
knowing he has used them himself
reprised his father's role
the same plea
passed down to another generation

its knowledge lost in the telling
made meaningless by time
by the warp and weft of things
by the drain-black

thirty-six   thirty-five   thirty-four

remembering is a scratched vinyl disc
replaying itself until the repeated phrase
is all there is

the melody forever lost

viii

the intrusion of a voice

what was that, Simpson

when do you know it's autumn, sir

when the path is strewn with the husks of nuts
broken in their futile fall to concrete
or crushed beneath the heavy-tread of impatient traffic
when the blend of broken shells and yellowing leaves
pattern puddles glossy with early morning rain

when coat collars go up

when your pace slows just a little
when keeping up gets harder
when breath gets shorter
like the lines of verse
you're able to read
without needing
to pause
for

breath

when longing is greater
when remembering is harder
even then
there's joy to be had

the unattended moment
the still point

listening for

unheard music

imagining the things you might have done
encapsulated in broken nut-shells

the husk of meaning

he writes four phrases on the chalkboard
knowing they are two steps away from understanding
two steps and perhaps forty years

then

you can't spend time twice

thirty-three   thirty-two   thirty-one

what can they know of autumn
these who have yet to experience the fulness of spring

and does it get cold, sir

cold

like ice on drainpipes
spittle frozen on pavements
ponds made solid enough for skating
one jumper
(or two jumpers)
thick with warp and weft
that heavy coat your granny bought
(and which you hate)
woolly hats and gloves
dug from chests of drawers

or the blood slowing in your veins
the trace of tartan behind your eyelids
where memory struggles to break through

or is that winter
where autumn is already over

and summer is a remembrance
and spring a myth

thirty   twenty-nine   twenty-eight

*not cold
but getting there*

ix

she asked

have you seen the water on the lake

the way sunlight streaks the surface
after a squall
elbowing between clouds
turning white horses to diamond
chasing waves to buffet the land

and now
the wind still up
water kissed by moonlight

do you remember when the park flooded

an overstatement
for the loss of a strip of land
in another lifetime

submerged beneath murky grey
the diamonds long gone

the innocence of gentle lapping
in and out
weft and warp

as if that were the way of things
to not be there
then be there
then gone

like a juggler's clubs pirouetting in the air

twenty-seven   twenty-six   twenty-five

wasn't it up to seven on the flood-gauge

footfalls echo in the memory

I didn't mean that year…

rhythm and crescendo
the coming and going of water
thrust first against the fell-sides
then down
falling down
into the waiting lake
as if it was there for that purpose
to gather   to nurture

but it was a bad year

who sees the moment
between flood and not-flood
who marks the first trespass
of water onto path or grass

twenty-four   twenty-three   twenty-two

when one thing turns to another
and pivots
about what

the still point

the unattended moment

for someone must be watching
chained to the warp and weft
the inevitability of pattern
searching the clouds for signs of a break
or the wind for another squall
knowing this might be the last time

to catch the white horses
as they whinny from their fathoms-deep stable
and gallop to the waiting shore

twenty-one   twenty   nineteen

it was
and old Mr. Loomis lost his caravan
parked it too close to the fence
just to get a better view

selfish

shellfish

syllables running on the tide of language
in and out
mistaken for diamonds
in the fret
syllables whinnying like horses
or mules
or asses
(who is there to tell the difference)

Old Mr. Loomis
serve him right

eighteen   seventeen   sixteen

then time takes over
the pied piper of closure

time for bed

you go, dear
I'll be along directly

as soon as he has stared
at the drain-black water on the lake a little longer
and re-imagined the things he saw
the white horses
the waiter
or the things he heard
about the accident
the story of the apple

the empty room echoes
to memory's footfall

switching off the light
is another ending
and he wonders
whether he will ever be as enchanted
as he once was

assuming that is what he felt

darkness smuggles
the pattern in the wallpaper
to somewhere else
somewhere beyond the lake
and the whispering wind

and he tries to recall it
the pattern
regular   rhythmical
woven into the fabric of his life

warp and weft
in and out

then an elsewhere voice

bring me some water would you

and the empty promise of tomorrow
looms invisibly before him

fifteen   fourteen   thirteen

x

swap duvets with the weather
always too light
(or too heavy)
just right only that first time
the time you snuggle down
too comfortable to read
cocooned in harvested down
wrapped in the warp and weft of cotton

is that cover new, dear

pattern suggesting a kind of
scandinavian tartan
and though the lines are rightly degreed
there is something in the shade

neither ochre nor burgundy
which suggests travesty
or impersonation

perhaps something woven
from circus cast-offs would be better
gaudy but cheerful

and as you allow yourself
to be swallowed whole
you remember that visit to the big-top
when you had been a child

risking enchantment

or so much later
at the restaurant when you ordered

what was it

or those times the park flooded
more or less
the water lapping at the land
the path
the empty pitches
from where caravans had been removed
as if that would ever be enough
to save them
or those that owned them

on the bedside table
a clock ticks

twelve   eleven   ten

but it is less like a clock
than the count of a juggler
the beat of an antique drum
there is something irregular
in the regularity
a secret
hidden in the gaps
between the sounds
or in the motion of the second-hand
that fragment of pause
when everything seems possible

and impossible at the same time

and you are left with
nothing
but the space in-between

listen

nine   eight   seven

can you hear the not-sound
the heavy-laden pause

the pregnancy in the moment
unattended
the point   still
which is neither one thing nor the other
where the world might turn
this way or that

in such moments

sense without enchantment

the rain might not come
the flood not happen
the car might not skid
the waiters remain resting on their elbows at the counter

you might not have to choose
between ribollita and whatever else it was
or argue about the flood gauge
the colours of tartan
the heaviness of the duvet

six five

but slip
instead
to sleep
or into autumn
or beyond autumn

is it cold, sir

colder than you could ever know
beyond the compensation of duvets
or tea

milk first! milk first!

untouched by the antics of clumsy clowns
unthreatened by the lion
undefeated by the juggler's
ability (or inability) to count

four   three

to see
what
just there
beyond   or in
night-time eyelids
the blood pulse of tartan
the weft and warp of veins

and just between the count

two

comes that point
that still moment

when

time is withdrawn

and the antique drum stops
and the world pivots
and the answer is almost there

one

crash

Beyond the Curtain

The Setting

Beyond the Curtain is a companion piece to *Crash*. Using the same character, it could be played as a second act: *Crash*, then an interval, then *Beyond the Curtain*.

The stage can be empty. Perhaps the space within which the actor reads could be draped in a heavy curtain. This space should not be the whole stage however, just a portion at the front.

If it was desired to make the setting more explicit, a coffin could be set to one side.

Note: *Beyond the Curtain* could easily be played as a double-hander (and might work better as such).

Beyond the Curtain

i

on the wrong side when the curtains closed
he listens to the music fade
hears voices numbed to silence
then waits   overwhelmed by darkness

and then waits some more

and for what
to be surprised by noise and light
and beaming faces

like that time when…

…there must have been such a once upon a time
but he cannot recall it now
nor imagine what sound is
brightness was

and though he has an inkling
the trace of an instinct
little is left
but

a dying fall

expectation once held him close
whispered the tune of possibilities
now silence is his sole companion
that and darkness

and so he waits some more
emptiness embraces him
nullifies his senses
sight and sound and touch
relegated to memory
and memory consigned to oblivion

it is worse than fog
than quicksand
than being swallowed whole
into the belly of some beast

worse than agony or despair

though how can he know as much
curtained off from feeling

what would he give
for a chink of light
the whisper of a familiar voice
the echo of a laugh from the child he once was

yet there is nothing
or there is something

an essence perhaps
ducking and diving to avoid being named
not a sense but a presence

or   better still   an absence

and now the void holds him close
enchants him with nonexistent music
deafens him with silence
clothes him in darkness

ii

his out-of-body voice speaks
seeking answers

is it like sleep
this silence
this darkness

not sleep
for sleep carries a promise
of dreaming
of waking

dreaming is the living of another life
a bonus awarded by imagination
when it is full
and seeks release
to overflow   somewhere

and dreams carry light
and sound
for do people not speak in dreams
all those people you left behind
on the other side of the curtain

those and more

in the mix of memory and desire
what do you see

a heap of broken images

that sleeping part of you
releasing the reins at last
endeavouring reassembly
to fix together the fractured jigsaw of your life
only to be forgotten
as you have forgotten
what

only everything

and there
invisible in the nowhere
is that residual instinct
(or inclination)
for which you'd like to find a name
an image
a sound

iii

what of this voice
the one you hear now
(or think you do)
proffering answers to unspoken questions
kidding you with dialogue
and the illusion of interaction

is that what keeps hope alive

if so
then cling to that
to hope if you must
give yourself up to pretence
allow whatever is left of you
what is not yet consumed by absence
(or that thing you cannot name)
allow it one final hurrah

pretend you can see
for one last time
pretend you can hear

believe
that what you can hear
(or what you once heard)
is not the wind in a chime
but

the rattle of bones

and that rhythm
(the echo from another time)
may or may not be
a juggler's counting
miscalculated in

the empty desolation

imagine
if you can
that this is your last chance
the last roll of the dice
even if they're loaded
weighted against you

and no matter the odds
the warnings from those who have gone before

the hollow men

still you wish
to juggle those dice in your hands
to hear the clicking of one against the other
to take that chance
(even though there is no gamble involved
as the outcome is surely certain)

and then
not knowing
what you need to roll
(or unconcerned by that)
release them
into the silence and darkness

and wait

for someone will tell you
(soundlessly)
how the dice have settled
the sum of the uppermost faces
the faces you cannot see
the spots you cannot count

peer into the darkness
as if you had eyes
as if there was light

listen to the silence
as if it were not there

and wait

for the irreconcilable dance
for the music of possibilities

iv

*is this like being born
coming into something new   afresh
the beginning of an adventure*

hardly
>   or not yet

for birth brings with it possibilities
explosions of sound and light
music in the silence
stars in the darkness

brings with it the challenge
of understanding
the chimera of comprehension
alluring
like a mirage
for a man thirsting in a desert

or the shadow of such a man

and now here you are
giving yourself up
to the pretence of things
the fantasy of making the mirage real

stretch out your hand
stretch out your imagined hand
and imagine the feel of a cup filled with water
can you recall   even imperfectly
the chill on the tips of your fingers
how water slipped from the cup
or ran across your skin
or those moments when a deluge
betrayed the bounds of the lake
to lap at the path   the grass
and changed its name from water
to flood

how strange
you might think
for the same thing
or two incarnations of the same thing
to have different names

water

flood

here
in the oblivion behind the curtain
should we seek names
for what we have lost

or is 'absence' sufficient

or should we endeavour to name it all
elements in an infinite list
where one thing leads to another

like water to flood

if so
count up or down
(like a juggler perhaps)
and without end
to arrive at the uncomfortable conclusion
that after all
life
is the only word that matters

a silent motto

the peg on which we hang everything
ignorant of what will happen
when the peg snaps
and

the human engine

stops
and the curtain closes
abandons us to this emptiness
this desolation

…

you say nothing
you can say nothing

yet what if such finality
were not that
but merely the next step
on an unforeseen journey
towards a different birth

a second coming if you will
delivery of a promise made
or the reward
for faithfulness
for taking on trust
what might have been a legend
what might still be a legend

v

*there was a time
when I could see things others could not
when they would look at me as I lay in bed
mixing concern with lack of understanding
while I
staring at them
(or over their shoulders)
was seeing as if for the first time
the nebulous   the unnamed
teasing me   challenging
saying*

*"now you are old enough
now you have come this far
you are ready for the final question
the conundrum
the puzzle of what we really are"*

or who you are

*have you seen them
have you been there
watched the shimmer at the edge of colours
or the reverberation of word-sound
like an echo imperfectly formed
as if within it
between syllables
might lay secrets and true meaning*

and their voice

*is a little like yours
now that you mention it*

then you have answered your own question

vi

comfort
is a matter of perspective

a plumped up cushion
in red velour
perhaps an irrelevance
if you cannot see it
(or feel it)

useless in the darkness

not quite a parting gift
it adorns the casket
a resting place for your skull
or an emblem of guilt
as if sewn into its fabric
in calligraphic embroidery
is an apology from others
for being left behind

or for being able to carry on
without you

they are
      both the comfort and the pillow
immaterial

if they could ask if you cared
if they made a difference
(the pillow or their words)
your answer would be the same

*I would prefer
my head weren't here at all*

perhaps you might conjure it
as payment for the ferryman
(should you believe in such mythology)
something to ease the passage
between here
                and somewhere else

always assuming…

indeed

'place your bets, place your bets!'

everywhere the gyre turns
a wheel spins
and a silver sphere bounces
in homage to chaos theory
the nip-and-tuck of chance

and if you could
you would remember where you placed your money
red or black
odds or evens
or zero
and all for what

to

disturb the universe

or perhaps to confirm
nothing more than superstition

rien na va plus

yet not   no more bets
but   all bets are off

the perpetually spinning wheel
persists in the peripheral vision
of those who walk away
to the sound of 'The Lark Ascending'
or 'In The Mood'
each of them
with one eye on email
the postman
or the lottery numbers

longing for something new
           life-changing

not a red velour cushion

vii

spin me another story

shall I

something like a bedtime fairy tale
whispered to a weary child
who needs comforting to sleep
even though this is the opposite

give me something to cling to
surprise me with a new truth
tell me that legends are real
and mythology fact
lift me up from this

from what

this red cushion
this nameless state

and make it all
                mean something

viii

some questions cannot be answered
no matter how well the words
are chosen
or woven

questions are spun as spiders spin webs
fragile   transparent
yet no matter how intricate
they can be easily brushed away
leaving us no longer
enchanted

questions beg to be heard
(or read)
always imperfect
missing context
poorly framed
or incomplete
impossible

sometimes not even verbal
(nor written)
a construct of the mind
like a mirage in an imagined desert

or then again
dredged from memory
that suddenly inadequate estuary
where silt has usurped water

or echoes of a child
(perhaps called Simpson)
who raises his hand to ask

is it cold, Sir

him knowing what he meant
all the while you did not

and yet you strive to find an answer
about cold and autumn
(where all this began)
to satisfy the chasm between you and he

and you talk of nuts and puddles
yellowing leaves
and breath

how autumn leads to winter
the multiplication of cold
on a journey that goes nowhere
except to a red velour cushion

is that the answer to the child's question
the answer you could not give
because you did not know
because you had not yet made the journey
beyond winter and into
what
a mirage within a mirage

the disconsolate chimera

perhaps

or perhaps you did know
but fear held your tongue

so let me ask it again
let me pretend I am Simpson
still young and innocent
my hand still aloft
where it will remain
until you have given me an answer
with which I can
do something
is it cold

it is

    nothing

ix

something and nothing perhaps
or nothing and something
which may be closer to the truth

the slightest spark
at the end of the longest tunnel
the faintest echo
at the end of a chain of echoes
a chain impossibly long
incalculable
even if you had imagination enough
to see to the end of things

and beyond

so it begins again
the thirst to learn
not the accumulation of facts
or data
nor of turning facts and data
into knowledge

but you should aspire to an unlearning
a dismantling
because all you once knew
was based on
enchantment

or watching acrobats
frozen in mid-air
the whip in mid-crack

the still point

the unattended moment

based on seeing or feeling
hearing or tasting
surrendering yourself
to the vagaries and weaknesses of the body
until via the cold
(of autumn and winter)
came the shortening of breath

the need for jumpers
and a countdown

but now there is none of that
just absence
everything there ever was
symbolised in a red velvet cushion

and everything there ever will be
embodied in a disembodied voice
which comes at you from nowhere
dragging you back
into memory
and regret

and forward

yes
perhaps
but did I not tell you to remove past hope

what do I need to do

to achieve what

in absence there is nothing
nothing you can say or do
because you have neither tongue nor body
nothing you can think or feel
because you have neither mind nor body

then what is left

perhaps everything

you think of liberation
in practical ways
of being freed from bonds
yet you were always free
except

except

except that you were always bound

once
(or once upon a time
if you prefer)
you walked

half-deserted streets

assuming they were thronged
by others just like you
mistaking their buffeting
as movement or progress or proof

and now
this new you
here
speaking without needing a voice

listening without needing ears
thinking and feeling
beyond
whatever it was you were

so what now

in that curtain
this darkness and silence
the cushion of red velvet
are symbols of

the end of the endless

or the end of enchantment

the silver ball
finally settling in the wheel
the dice finally coming to rest
the coin no longer spinning

do you imagine all this to be
                            judgement
an answer
the weighing of what you were
measured in silence and darkness
and the nap of red velvet

what else can it be

perhaps it is also the end of the beginning
the alarum which trumpets
the resurrection of the soul
inviolable
impossibly possible

perhaps it is that

we must weigh
what you may yet become
not who you once were

essence not absence

x

when I was a child
I used to dream of journeys
taking trains or cars or boats
from one place to the next
the starting point
was always known
but the destination
                changed
                        always
the route   deviated

the plan was not to be trusted

was it as if places had assumed

deliberate disguises

you might say that

*I was never where I expected to be
but somehow always lost
or always losing someone
thwarted by forces
I assumed were dark
and to which I gave dark names*

for such is our response to fear

*and I would dive headlong
back into dream after dream
seeking resolution
seeking a replay with a different outcome
where I was no longer lost
shipwrecked
alone*

and now

now

are you on a journey now
or do you feel scared
frightened
lost

can you resolve

the heap of broken images

find in the lay-lines of your life
colours and sounds
the clues left for you
a breadcrumb trail
woven into the fabric of your dream's end

I can see nothing

I do not recall the journey
nor how I got here
nor know where here is
nor where I was going

is that being lost

no
it is being found

it is coming home

Acknowledgements

Crash was first published in a pocket-size volume by Coverstory books (2023).

The small quotes from the poetry of T.S.Eliot are taken from *Collected Poems, 1909-1962* by T.S.Eliot, Faber and Faber (1963).

Quotes are also taken from *Selected Poems: 1976-2022* by Ian Gouge, Coverstory books (2022).